The Rockwool Foundation Research Unit

The impact of changes in life-stage on time allocations in Denmark: a panel study 2001-2009

Jens Bonke

University Press of Southern Denmark
Odense 2012

The impact of changes in life-stage on time allocations in Denmark:
a panel study 2001-2009

Study Paper No. 42

Published by:
© The Rockwool Foundation Research Unit and
University Press of Southern Denmark

Copying from this book is permitted only within
institutions that have agreements with CopyDan,
and only in accordance with the limitations laid
down in the agreement

Address:
The Rockwool Foundation Research Unit
Sølvgade 10, 2.tv
DK-1307 Copenhagen K

Telephone   +45 33 34 48 00

Fax   +45 33 34 48 99

E-mail   forskningsenheden@rff.dk

Home page   www.rff.dk

ISBN 978-87-90199-70-8
ISSN 0908-3979
May 2012
Print run: 350
Printed by   Specialtrykkeriet Viborg

Price: 60.00 DKK, including 25% VAT

Contents

Introduction 6

2 Data.. 8

3 Descriptive Statistics... 9

4 Empirical strategy.. 13

5 Results... 14

    5.1 Multinomial ordinary least squares results 14

    5.2 Fixed effects results...................................... 17

6 Conclusion 21

References 23

The impact of changes in life-stage on time allocations in Denmark: a panel study 2001-2009

Jens Bonke[1] *

Abstract This paper investigates the relation between women and men's life stages and their time allocation: paid work, household work, childcare and leisure time, and, in particular, how this allocation changes when moving from one stage to another stage. We use a new Danish panel dataset merged with Danish administrative register data, which allows for analyzing the impact of individual, endogenous characteristics of the respondents such as preferences for doing specific activities. We find that the labour supply of fathers to preschool children is not different from that of young men without children, while there is a negative correlation between mothers to preschool children and young women's labour supply. Comparing fathers and mothers to school children with those to preschool children, we find a positive correlation in both sexes labour supply. However, fixed effects estimations do not result in a reduction in mothers, nor in fathers, to preschool children's labour supply indicating that there are some inborn characteristics for the other life-stage changes which are not revealed by doing ordinary cross-sectional analyses.

Keywords: Life-stage; Time-allocation; Fixed effects
JEL Classifications: I10; I12

[1] Rockwool Foundation Research Unit, Sølvgade 10, 2.tv., 1307 Copenhagen, Denmark.
* Corresponding author: Jens Bonke; address: Rockwool Foundation Research Unit, Sølvgade 10 [2tv], 1307 Copenhagen, Denmark. E-mail: jb@rff.dk; Tel: +45 3334 4804; Fax: +45 3334 4899

Introduction

There is a number of investigations about the relationship between work and leisure time, and how children impact on this relationship, se e.g. Bonke (2009a). Hence, the implication of having children besides time spent on child care also means more household work and investments in durables such as cars and bigger houses. Although large subsidies are given to child families directly as child allowances and indirectly as public subsidies to child care facilities, see Bonke (2009b), and financial markets allow for "income-smoothing", i.e. savings before having children and lending and down spending afterwards (Bonke & Browning, 2011), fathers are found to work more and mothers less than men and women without children (Deding & Larsen, 2008). This redistribution of time within the family, however, allows for keeping household income intact while the child(ren) grows up.

Also formatting a couple without having children in first case impact on men and women's time allocation, although to a much lesser extent than having children. This is primarily due to a gendered distribution of household work with the wife contributing more than the husband, which might be explained by different preferences for and productivity in the doing of household work. Later on in the empty nest life-stage, the gendered contribution to household work in previous life-stages is prevailing, probably because the division of labor in the child-life stage continues due to established gender roles and experiences obtained during that life-stage.

In this paper we investigate how Danish men and women's time allocation vary over different life-stages in the period 2001-2008/09. Hence, we compare the time spend on paid work, household work, leisure, sleep and child care of men and women, respectively, living as 1) singles without children with couples without children and wives under the age of 45, 2) couples without children and wives under the age of 45 with parents to children under 7 years of age, 3) parents to children under 7 years of age to parents with youngest child between 7 and 17 years of age, 4) parents with youngest child between 7 and 17 years of age with couples without children and wives over the age of 44 years, and, finally, 5) couples without children and wives over the age of 44 years with singles without children and over 44 years of age. Besides the problem of being sure that these groups represent consecutive life-stages – singles are also to be found in between couple life-stages – the information rely on cross-sectional data for which reason the men and women in the different life-stages are not the same. To take this into account we also calculated the shift in time allocation for the very same people going from one life-stage to another life-stage due to panel-data information for the period 2001-2008/09.

Following, Robinson and Godbey (1997) several factors contribute to determine how people spend their time. Besides biological factors (age, sex, race), role factors (marriage, parenthood), status factors (education, occupation and income), environmental factors (urbanicity, region, housing type) and temporal factors (day of the week, season and year) are all of importance for the allocation on ones time. Together with these life-style characteristics, individual preferences and choices are explaining the actual time allocation within a zero-sum property to time with 24 hours as the ultimate constraint on human activity (Joyce and Steward, 1999) and finite resource (Robinson, 1997).

Life course transitions are important indicators of social and behavioural changes in women and men's life (Fast & Frederick, 2004), and also determinants of quality of life outcomes. Being married, having children, etc. all represent life course events, which are judged by societal expectations about role content across the lifespan, not to mention the way peoples spend their time. Hence, time-allocation and consumption patterns are probably the most revealing way of showing who people are and which group in society they belong to.

The usual chronological order of life course transitions implies that one goes from youth to adulthood, which generally occurs between the ages of 15 to 29, and implies economic and social independence of parents and the schooling system, and the entering of the labour market. The next transition is from singlehood to marriage/cohabitation with coordination of time-use and sharing of income as one of the most prominent changes for both partners. This is for the great majority followed by parenthood which even more than partnering has important consequences for women and men's behaviour, allocation of household and paid work and individual well-being (Coltraine and Ishi-Kuntz, 1992). The empty nest stage, when children have left home, is affecting the way leisure time is spend more than the amount of labour supplied to the labour market, and the retirement from the labour market is obviously a very radical change in peoples time-allocation with many unanswered question due to increasing life expectancies, population aging and feminization of the older population.

In between these life stages occurs singlehood with and without children due to more divorces and remarriages, and the formerly life course considered as a sequence of discrete events that happened to people in a relatively linear fashion at more or less fixed and prescribed times are not any more the general rule. Life course patterns are now more diverse, the timing of transitions less precise and universal, and the life course to be considered as an extended and complex process for modern people.

Despite this complexity in life course movements we here focus on the more traditional ones: singlehood, young couples, parents to preschool children, parents to school children, older couples, and old-age singles, and the activities we address are paid work, household work, child care, leisure and sleep.

The results indicate that having children only affects women's time spent on the labour market not that of men, and that the time spent on children for women is taken from paid work as well as from leisure, while for men time spent on children primarily goes from their leisure time.

2 Data

The data used stem from the Danish Time Use Panel Survey 2001–2008/09 (DTUP), which is a merged dataset of The Danish Time Use Survey 2001 and The Danish Time and Consumption Survey 2008/09 (Bonke & Fallesen, 2010) both drawn randomly among 18-74-olds from administrative registers held by Statistics Denmark. Respondents in 2001 were asked also to participate in 2008/2009 – up to the age of 74 years – by giving diary information on the same weekday and weekend day. In the unbalanced panel all individuals with diary information on a weekday and a weekend day were included: 4828 men and 5153 women. In the balanced panel used for the fixed effect estimations the sample consisted of 1247 men and 1517 women.

The basic information in both waves of the panel about family relations, socioeconomic status, educational level, and average number of working hours was conducted through telephone or internet-interviews followed up by the completion of two time use diaries one for a weekday and one for a weekend day in 2001 as well as in 2008/09.

In the diaries the respondent reported the primary activity s/he was engaged in during the day. In 2008/09 there were 34 pre-coded activities to choose between opposite to 2001, where the respondents were asked to report the activities done in their own words, i.e. post-coding. Table A1 includes a list of the activities used in this paper. Because of the inclusion of a unique identifier in DTUP we were able to merge with administrative register data in Statistics Denmark, which increased available information considerably. The combination of survey and administrative register also made it possible to test for sample selection – e.g. unemployed and those who are immigrants are underrepresented – and through a weighing-procedure make the DTUP representative for the population as a whole.

Information on employment status and educational background stem from administrative registers, where employment is included as a binary variable: employed versus un- or non-employed. Education refers to the longest completed course of education and we distinguish between individuals having completed a further education – short-course further education (less than 3 years), medium-course further education (3 to 4 years), and long-course further education (more than 4 years) – and individuals with vocational or no education. Also age was added as a control variable in the regressions.

3 Descriptive Statistics

Table 1 shows descriptive statistics for the sample of married/cohabitating men and women, respectively, for the pooled sample and for each of the years 2001 and 2008/2009. We find that time spent on child care among fathers increased between 2001 and 2008/2009: average time spent was 0,28 hours a day in 2001 and 0,34 hours in 2008/09. For household work, we found an increase in men's time and a decrease in women's time devoted to that activity. Time spent on paid work decrease for both men and women during the period 2001-2008/09, while awake leisure time increased for both sexes: more for women than for men. Finally, we found that men and women slept nearly 0,2 hours a night more in 2008/09 than in 2001.

Table 1 Descriptive statistics. Mean and standard deviation in parentheses. Men and women. 2001 and 2008/9 samples.

	Pooled 2001, 2008/9	2001	2008	Pooled 2001, 2008/9	2001	2008
	Men			Women		
	Means (St. dev.)					
Childcare[1] (Hours/day)	0,32 (0,87)	0,28 (0,67)	0,34 (0,94)	0,57 (1,24)	0,58 (1,18)	0,57 (1,26)
Household work[1] (Hours/day)	2,31 (1,98)	2,26 (1,73)	2,33 (2,07)	3,03 (1,91)	3,10 (1,76)	2,99 (1,97)
Paid work[1] (Hours/day)	3,84 (3,27)	3,99 (3,13)	3,77 (3,32)	2,83 (2,84)	2,97 (2,72)	2,76 (2,90)
Leisure[1] (Hours/day)	8,94 (3,01)	8,82 (2,81)	8,99 (3,09)	8,76 (2,81)	8,42 (2,56)	8,93 (2,91)
Sleep[1] (Hours/day)	7,86 (1,53)	7,72 (1,34)	7,92 (1,60)	8,09 (1,45)	7,95 (1,32)	8,16 (1,51)
	Per cent					
Single wo/child, <45 years	0,16 (0,37)	0,19 (0,39)	0,15 (0,36)	0,12 (0,33)	0,18 (0,39)	0,09 (0,29)
Couple wo/child, woman <45 years	0,09 (0,29)	0,14 (0,35)	0,07 (0,25)	0,09 (0,29)	0,14 (0,35)	0,07 (0,26)
Couple, child <7 years	0,14 (0,35)	0,14 (0,35)	0,14 (0,35)	0,14 (0,35)	0,14 (0,35)	0,14 (0,35)

Couple, child 7-17 years	0,16 (0,37)	0,13 (0,34)	0,17 (0,38)	0,17 (0,37)	0,15 (0,35)	0,18 (0,38)
Couple wo/child, woman >44 years	0,35 (0,48)	0,32 (0,47)	0,36 (0,48)	0,35 (0,48)	0,28 (0,45)	0,38 (0,49)
Single wo/child, >44 years	0,10 (0,30)	0,07 (0,26)	0,11 (0,31)	0,13 (0,33)	0,10 (0,30)	0,14 (0,34)
	100.0	100.0	100.0	100.0	100.0	100.0
Further education[2] (1/0)	0,33 (0,47)	0,30 (0,46)	0,34 (0,47)	0,44 (0,50)	0,38 (0,48)	0,47 (0,50)
Age (years)	46,43 (16,06)	43,28 (15,23)	47,78 (14,78)	46,04 (14,62)	41,86 (14,67)	48,00 (14,18)
Employed/ un-, non-employed	0,71 (0,45)	0,70 (0,46)	0,72 (0,45)	0,64 (0,48)	0,64 (0,48)	0,64 (0,48)
N:	2983-2935	897-982	2086-2043	3235-3068	1030-984	2205-2084

[1] See Table A1

[2] Short-course further education (less than 3 years), medium-course further education (3 to 4 years), and long-course further education (more than 4 years) versus vocational or no education.

Note: Sample consist of respondents in the DTUS 2001 and 2008/2009.

Time use variables are weighted averages of one weekday and one weekend day.

These changes in time spent on the different activities are distributed differently over the life stages (Figure 1-5). Hence, the decrease in paid work is caused by considerably fewer hours worked by late life-stage women and men, which more than out-weighted an increase in early life-stage women and men, with the most marked change over men's life-stages between 2001 and 2008/09.

The changes in household work were nearly parallel for all life-stage men and women, with the exception of mothers to preschool children, who spent considerably less time on this activity in 2008/09 than in 2001. Child care, on the other hand, increased for mothers to preschool children, while it decreased for such fathers. For mother and fathers to schoolchildren nearly no changes in child care took place within the study period.

Figure 1-5. The distribution of activities over life-stages. 2001 and 2008/09.

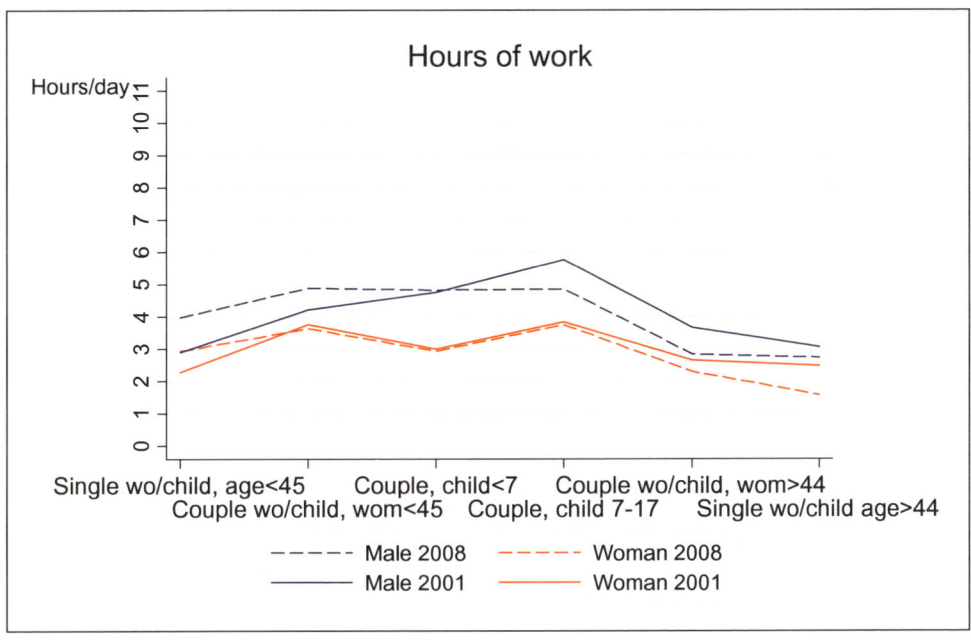

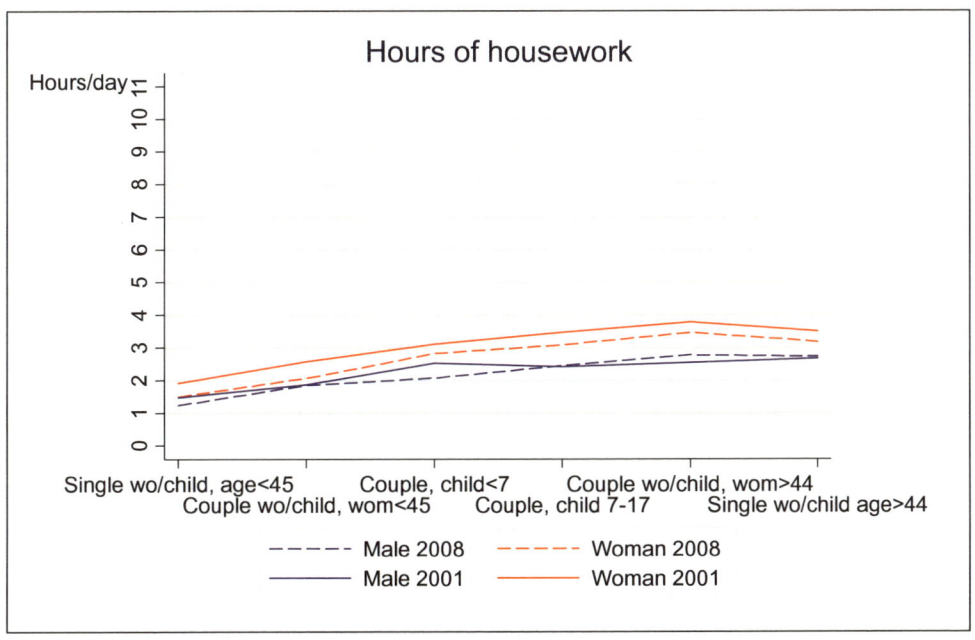

12 *Descriptive Statistics*

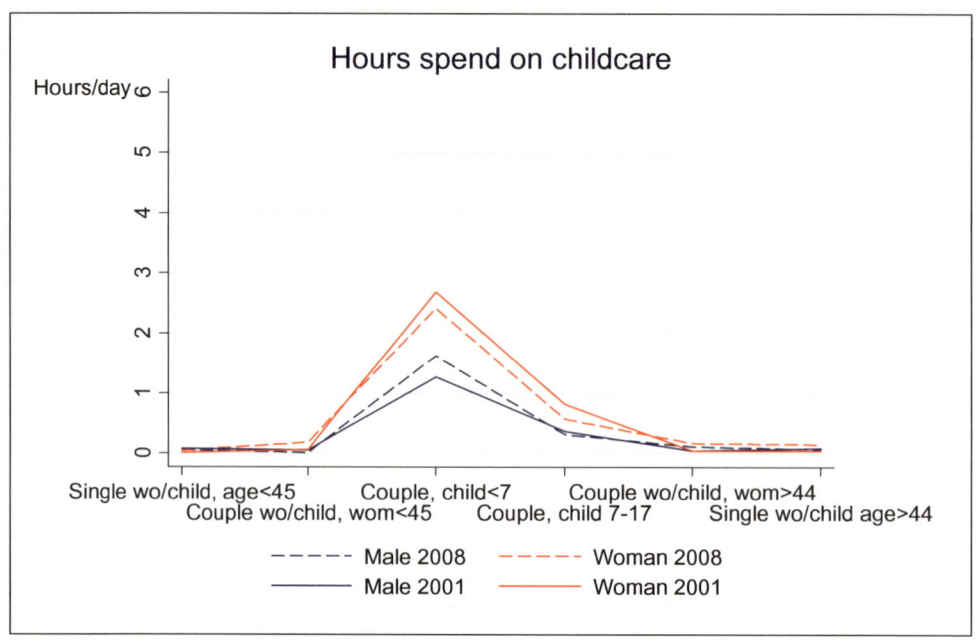

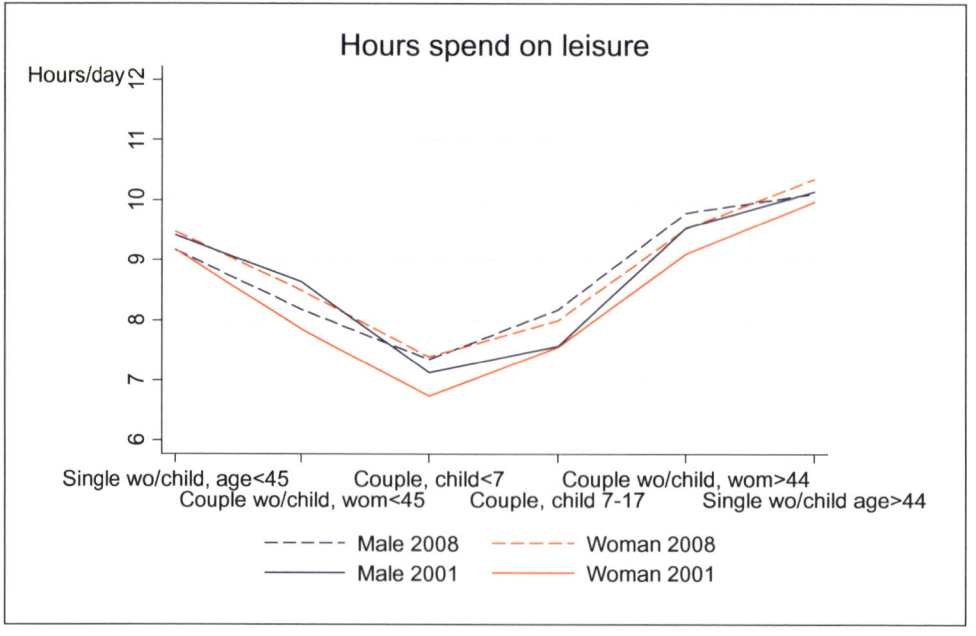

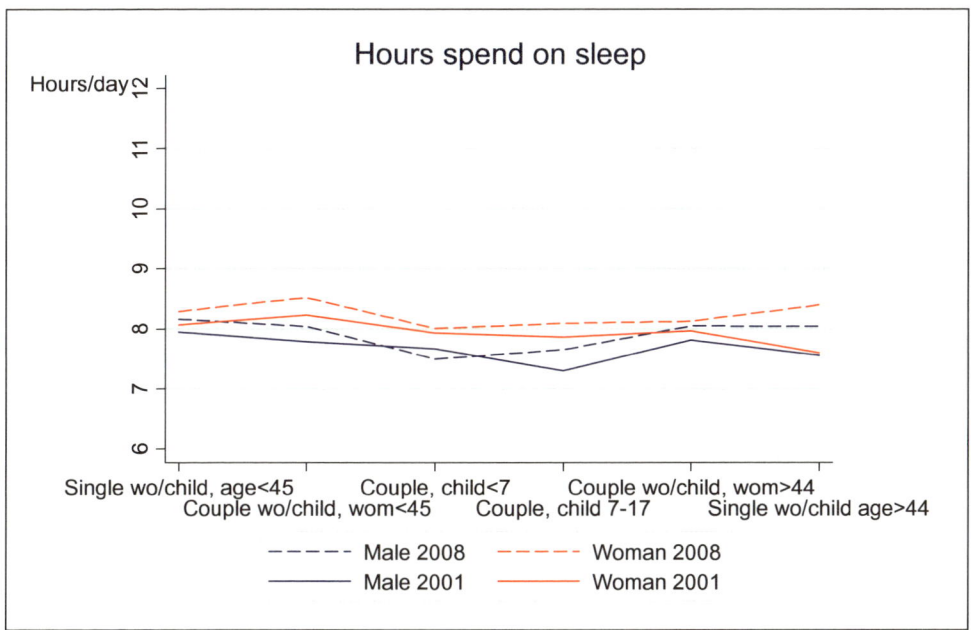

For women at all life-stages they experienced more awake leisure, whereas this happened only to men with children and older married men without children. For older, single men awake leisure time remained virtually the same, and for early life-stage single or partnered men more awake leisure was obtained within the last 10 years.

The more sleep obtained in the period was first of all to the benefit of women, who all slept more hours in 2001 than in 2008/09. For men the same happened except for fathers to preschool children, who slept fewer hours in 2008/09.

4 Empirical strategy

The paper analyses the effect of life-stage changes on time allocation, such as time spent on paid work, household work, leisure, sleep and child care. We apply a model for each activity and for men and women, separately.

The form of the equation is the following:

(1) $T_{jit} = X_{it}\beta_1 + \beta_2 LS_{it} + u_{it}$

Where T_{jit} is time spent on the activity j at time t done by individual I, X is a vector of different correlates, LS indicates life stages, and u is the error term. The error term has two components: An individual effect, ε_i, which represents unobserved fixed characteristics of the individual and a random error, γ_{it}, which is assumed to be normally distributed. Hence, the error term has the form:

(2) $u_{it} = \varepsilon_i + \gamma_{it}$

The problem is that a correlation between life-stage and the error term u, will bias the β_2-estimates in a OLS-regression, because it does not take the impact of unobserved characteristics into consideration. That is, the individual's time allocation is affected by having children, i.e. earning an income and thus doing paid work, and the activities are decided simultaneously. Furthermore, unobserved time invariant characteristics correlated with life-stage might also correlate with time spent on different activities. For instance, individuals who discount the future will be less likely to have children and perhaps more likely to work many hours at the labour market, which implies that the unobserved time invariant component in the error term, ε, and life-stage will be negatively correlated, and the coefficient β_2 will be biased downwards.

In the following, we begin by using the unbalanced, pooled sample for the years 2001 and 2008/09 and control for clustering, because some respondents participated in both waves/surveys. Life-stages are included as a categorical variable, where the reference-group changes to function as "departure" life-stages positioned right before the "arriving" life-stage. The implication is that all the observations are included in the estimations independently of the life-stage transition under consideration. Then we use the balanced panel doing fixed effects estimations to deal with the bias that may arise due to the correlation between unobserved characteristics and life-stage.

5 Results

5.1 Multinomial ordinary least squares results

Table 2 shows the multinomial ordinary least square (OLS) results of equation (1) applied on pair-wise groups of consecutive life-stages (the full estimations are available on request). In Panel A we find the results for men and in Panel B the results for women. The columns 1–5 show the results on equation (1) for the outcomes time spent on childcare, household work, paid work, leisure and sleep. In addition to the life-stage variable, we include educational background, employment, age and a dummy variable for year in the OLS specification. Although life-stages are defined by, among other things, age, we include this variable to delimit the age-effect on time-allocations when we compare two nearby life-stage groups being single individuals with younger couples without children. Also employment – employed versus non-employed – and educational background – further education versus shorter or no education – vary with life-stages, but again, by including these binary variables, we end up by getting a "purer" effect or correlation between life-stage changes and changes in time-allocation.

Table 2 Multinomial ordinary least squares estimation of time spent on childcare, household work, paid work, leisure and sleep. Adjusted for education, employment, age and year. Men and women. Pooled sample 2001-2008/09

	Childcare	Household work	Paid work	Leisure	Sleep
	Marginal effects (Std error)				
	Men				
Couple wo/child, woman <45 years vs . single wo/child, aged <45	-0,0242	0,434**	0,237	-0,556**	-0,0405
	(0,06)	(0,15)	(0,20)	(0,21)	(0,12)
Couple, child <7 years vs. couple wo/child, woman <45	1,467***	0,303*	-0,315	-0,881***	-0,333**
	(0,06)	(0,15)	(0,2)	(0,21)	(0,12)
Couple, child 7-17 years vs. couple, child < 7 years	-1,193***	-0,115	0,456*	0,461*	-0,0187
	(0,05)	(0,14)	(0,18)	(0,19)	(0,11)
Couple wo/child, woman >44 years vs. couple, child 7-17 years	-0,263***	-0,456***	-0,0909	0,346+	0,147
	(0,05)	(0,13)	(0,17)	(0,18)	(0,10)
Single wo/ child, aged >44 vs. couple wo/child, woman >44 years	-0,0114	0,0686	-0,0588	0,313+	-0,076
	(0,05)	(0,12)	(0,17)	(0,17)	(0,10)
N			2949		
R-sq	0,3191	0,0998	0,3976	0,2279	0,0526
	Woman				
Couple wo/child, woman <45 years vs . single wo/child, aged <45	0,220**	0,539***	0,346+	-0,913***	0,284*
	(0,07)	(0,14)	(0,18)	(0,20)	(0,12)
Couple, child <7 years vs. couple wo/child, woman <45	2,468***	0,492***	-0,939***	-1,088***	-0,401***
	(0,07)	(0,14)	(0,17)	(0,19)	(0,11)
Couple, child 7-17 years vs. couple, child < 7 years	-1,697***	-0,124	0,632***	0,574**	0,0675
	(0,06)	(0,12)	(0,16)	(0,18)	(0,10)

Results

Couple wo/child, woman >44 years vs. couple, child 7-17 years	-0,373***	-0,617***	0,213	0,382*	-0,0973
	(0,06)	(0,12)	(0,15)	(0,17)	(0,10)
Single wo/ child, aged >44 vs. couple wo/child, woman >44 years	0,00765	-0,406***	-0,0173	0,404**	0,048
	(0,05)	(0,10)	(0,13)	(0,14)	(0,08)
N			3115		
R	0,4566	0,1702	0,3768	0,2234	0,0257

Note: clustered for same individual observations in 2001 and 2008/09
+ $p<0.10$, * $p<0.05$, ** $p<0.01$, *** $p<0.001$

The results show a significant association for women between moving from singlehood to parenthood and time spent on childcare, although there are no home-living children in either of the two life-stages. The explanation probably is that some people have children from previous relationships – or children from the present relationship who have left home – on whom they spent some time: less if single men are compared with partnered men and more, when comparing single women with partnered women.

Also household work increases when men and women are formatting a partnership. However, only women's paid work is affected by this life-stage change, maybe to be seen as the woman's economic contribution to establishing and investing in a new home. Together with the increase in household work – and also in sleep – women have to pay in terms of an hour's reduction in time spent on leisure time. Hence, younger, married/cohabiting men without children have 0.6 hours more daily leisure than younger, single men without children, and for women the difference is 1.0 hour in favor of the singles.

The time devoted to childcare in families with children below 7 years of age is primarily taken from leisure and sleep. Two-third of the 1.5 hours fathers to preschool children spent on their children – there might also be older children in such families – is taken from leisure, while only 40 percent of women's 2.5 hours childcare come from that source. Also 0.3-0.4 hours of sleep are given up by men and women when having a child, partly due to more housework to be done for both partners – 0.3 versus 0.5 hours. Besides the price to be paid in terms of leisure, women giving birth also reduce their paid work, which is 0.9 hour less for younger women without children. For men no such pay is actualized as they work the same number of hours whether they have younger children or no children.

For fathers to school-age children paid work is 0.5 hours longer than for fathers to preschool children, and for mothers the difference is 0.6 hours, implying that when children grow older some of the reduction in mothers' paid work related to having a child is regained when the child reach school age. For fathers it seems to be the time, where they have the opportunity to increase their paid working hours, which was not so much the case, when the child was younger. Also a great part of leisure is regained for father and mothers, when their children grow older and less caring time is required: that is, fathers to school children spent 1.2 hour less per day taking care of their children, relatively to the 1.5 hours increase when going from no children to having preschool children. For mothers to school children the same figures were 1.7 hours relatively to 2.5 for the first transition. For leisure time, fathers and mothers regained about 50 per cent of what they had to give up when having their first and younger child.

Obviously, the great majority of time spent on child care disappears when children leave home and empty nests appear. For both women and men also the time devoted to household work decreases significantly and to nearly the same extend, which allows for 20 minutes more leisure time per day for both sexes, when the last child leaves the home.

Finally, we find that for women the time spent on household work is different between those being in a partnership and those living on their own. Hence, household work declines with 0.4 hours a day, while no such difference is found for men in the two life-stages. For both sexes, however, 0.3-0.4 hours of leisure are gained by living on ones own relatively to have a partner in old-age. These changes are not because of older single women's older age relatively to older women's in a partnership – women survive men – as we control for age-differentials between the two groups.

For all these comparison we have here and there talked about transitions, although the different life-style groups are populated by different people and not the same ones, as is the case in the following fixed effects analyses.

5.2 Fixed effects results

The problems occurring when life-stages are endogenous was described in section 4 focusing on the simultaneous determination and the presence of a third unobserved factor correlating with both time allocated to the specific activities and to life-stage: a simultaneous preference for being married and spending time together with a partner. This problem cannot be solved when doing OLS-regressions, whereas fixed effects estimations take care of the presence of

Table 3 Life-stages and time allocation in Denmark. Panel data 2001-2008/09. Fixed effects estimations adjusted for education, and unemployment.

	Single wo/child, aged <45 → couple wo/child, woman <45 years			Couple wo/child, woman <45 → Couple, child <7 years			Couple, child <7 years → couple, child 7-17 years			Couple, child 7-17 years → couple wo/child, woman >44 years			couple wo/child, woman >44 years → single wo/ child, aged >44		
	2001 Means	2008 Means	Coeff. (t-statistics)	2001 Means	2008 Means	Coeff. (t-statistics)	2001 Means	2008 Means	Coeff. (t-statistics)	2001 Means	2008 Means	Coeff. (t-statistics)	2001 Means	2008 Means	Coeff. (t-statistics)
						Hours:minutes/day Men									
Childcare	..	..	..	00:00	02:02	2,029*** (-7,69)	01:15	00:25	-0,811*** (-6,96)	00:19	00:02	-0,285** (-3,16)	..	..	..
Household work	..	..	..	01:42	01:56	0,214 (0,78)	02:17	02:23	0,0345 (0,16)	02:13	02:32	0,165 (0,52)	..	..	..
Paid work	..	..	..	04:50	05:12	-0,205 (-0,40)	05:23	05:32	0,183 (0,44)	06:02	05:28	-0,209 (-0,04)	..	..	..
Leisure time	..	..	..	08:35	06:40	-1,784*** (-3,65)	07:04	07:36	0,497 (1,36)	07:35	07:53	0,0806 (0,23)	..	..	..
Sleep	..	..	..	07:27	07:19	-0,0828 (-0,30)	07:25	07:32	0,163 (1,03)	00:14	07:31	0,322+ (1,91)	..	..	..
N	16			54			73			64			6		

Results   19

	Single wo/child, aged <45 → couple wo/child, woman <45 years			Couple wo/child, woman <45 → Couple, child <7 years			Couple, child <7 years → couple, child 7-17 years			Couple, child 7-17 years → couple wo/child, woman >44 years			couple wo/child, woman >44 years → single wo/child, aged >44		
	2001 Means	2008 Means	Coeff. (t-statistics)	2001 Means	2008 Means	Coeff. (t-statistics)	2001 Means	2008 Means	Coeff. (t-statistics)	2001 Means	2008 Means	Coeff. (t-statistics)	2001 Means	2008 Means	Coeff. (t-statistics)
						Women									
						Hours:minutes/day									
Childcare	00:00	00:22	0,346 (0,91)	00:07	02:39	2,405*** (8,11)	02:10	00:41	−1,311*** (−7,80)	00:31	00:06	−0,402*** (−4,17)	..	..	..
Household work	01:50	02:03	−0,0541 (−0,09)	02:10	02:44	0,423 (1,3)	02:58	03:10	0,269 (1,15)	03:28	03:03	−0,426 (−1,58)	..	..	..
Paid work	01:53	03:40	1,323 (1,36)	03:49	03:09	−1,180+ (−1,95)	03:42	04:02	0,0196 (0,05)	03:40	04:20	0,742* (2,00)	..	..	..
Leisure time	08:14	08:05	0,0162 (0,01)	08:09	07:01	−0,908+ (−1,98)	06:48	07:40	0,823* (2,34)	07:54	07:59	−0,00307 (−0,01)	..	..	..
Sleep	08:19	08:38	0,998+ (1,95)	08:03	07:52	−0,222 (−0,87)	07:49	07:58	0,218 (1,28)	07:56	07:49	−0,125 (−0,69)	..	..	..
N	24			60			72			74			17		

+ p<0.1, * p<0.05, ** p<0.01, *** p<0.001

Note: 2008-weights, Statistics Denmark .. <20 obs.

unobserved characteristics, i.e. the time invariant component in the error term, ε_i, being correlated with life-stage, producing consistent estimates of the effect of life-stage on time spent on specific activities.

Also fixed effects estimates cause problems, because they are sensitive to measurement errors and might bias fixed effects estimates downwards. Although we do not believe that the measure of age, civil status and children implies measurement error, the time use variables might include errors depending on the activities. For example, unobserved variables might influence both having children and time spent on child care, and these unobserved variables may vary over time – quantities have been converted into qualities with fewer children and more time spent per child (Bonke, 2009a; Bianchi, 2000; Bianchi et al., 2006). Furthermore, relatively few of those with time diary information in both 2001 and 2008/2009 changed life-stage status from 2001 to 2008/9 giving a relatively small balanced sample.

Nonetheless, we do fixed effects estimations together with OLS-estimations because of an expected relationship between life-stage and unobserved fixed characteristics causing a potential problem when applying equation (1). That is, there might be a selection into marriage and the same for having children, although nearly 90 per cent of Danish women have at least one child within their fertile period.

Table 3 reports the fixed effects estimates with the results for men found in Panel A and the results for women in Panel B. The control variable age drops out of the estimation, because it is fixed over time. Column 3 presents the fixed effects estimates on the effect of life-stage transitions on paid work, household work, child care, leisure and sleep. Compared with the earlier OLS results, there are more fixed-effects-estimations, which cannot be done due to attrition. Hence, there are two few observations to follow younger men into marriage/cohabitation (16 obs.), and the same holds for men and women's transitions from marriage to the older singlehood stage (6 and 17 obs.). Moreover, the fixed effects results show fewer significant parameter estimates, and among those being significant the parameter estimates are in some cases higher than when doing OLS-regressions.

The fixed effects estimates in Table 3, Column 3, show that among men, having a child means a 2.0 hour increase in time spent on child care and for women 2.4 hours, which is 0.6 and 0.1 hours more than found in the OLS-regressions. When the child grows older and become a school child the fixed effects for women and men are smaller than that obtained by OLS-estimates. Finally, when children leave the parents, the fixed effects for the mother as well as for the father are equal to the OLS-estimates. The higher fixed effect estimates for the first transistion points to fixed unobserved factors positively correlating with life-stages with children biasing the OLS estimates in Table 2 downwards, whereas this is not the case for the other transitions, when looking at time spent on child care.

For men and women there are no effects of life-stage transitions on time spent on household work, which is in contrast with the OLS estimates, where positive correlations between early life-stage changes and negative between late life-stage changes were found. The positive OLS-estimates for paid work, when comparing women and men with preschool children with women and men with school children, disappear in the fixed effect estimates. However, the significant and negative OLS-estimates for women with preschool children relative to women without children, becomes larger when following the same women's transition from the second to the first stage. Also the OLS-estimate of older couples without children compared with women with school children is smaller – and not signifikacant – than the fixed-effect estimate for the very same transition. The suggestion is that some fixed unobserved factors positively correlating with life-stages biasing the OLS-estimates downwards, when the focus is on time spent at the labor market.

Moreover, the OLS-estimates for leisure time is found of nearly the double size relatively to the fixed-effect estimates for younger men without children compared with fathers to young children, while there is no such difference between the two estimates for women having children and living with children becoming older.

Finally, when children leave the home men increase their sleep significantly, which was not the case when looking at the OLS-estimates. We also found that young single women increases their sleep considerably – 1 hour per day – when being married/cohabiting, while the OLS-estimate only showed an increase of 0.3 hours.

6 Conclusion

This paper offers new insight on life-stage differences in time allocation, i.e. time spent on paid work, household work, child care, leisure and sleep. The results indicate that having children only affects women's time spent on the labour market not that of men, and that the time spent on children for women is taken from paid work as well as from leisure, while for men time spent on children primarily goes from their leisure time.

A new Danish time use panel dataset for the period 2001–2008/2009 gives the opportunity to compare OLS estimates with fixed effects of life-stage changes on men and women's time spent on different activities: Paid work, household work, child care, leisure and sleep.

The fixed effects estimates show that among men, having a child means 2.0 hours of time care and for women 2.4 hours, which is 0.6 and 0.1 hours more than found in the OLS-regressions. When the child grows older and become a school child the fixed effect for women is smaller than that obtained by OLS-estimates, and when children leave the parents the fixed effects for the mother as well as for the father are equal to the OLS-estimates. The higher fixed effect estimates for the first transistion points to fixed unobserved factors positively correlating with life-stages with children biasing the OLS estimates downwards, whereas this is not the case for the other transitions, when looking at time spent on child care.

For men and women there are no effects of life-stage transitions on time spent on household work, which is in contrast with the OLS estimates, where positive correlations between early life-stage changes and negative between late life-stage changes were found. The positive OLS-estimates for paid work, when comparing women and men with preschool children with women and men with school children, disappear in the fixed effect estimates. However, the significant and negative OLS-estimates for women with preschool children relative to women without children, becomes larger when following the same women's transition from the second to the first stage. Also the OLS-estimate of older couples without children compared with women with school children is smaller than the fixed-effect estimate for the very same transition. Again, the suggestion is that some fixed unobserved factors positively correlating with life-stages biasing the OLS-estimates downwards, when the focus is on time spent at the labor market.

Compared with the OLS results there are too few observations to follow younger men into marriage/cohabitation, and the same holds for men and women's transitions from marriage to the older singlehood stage, due to attrition. Moreover, the fixed effects results show fewer significant parameter estimates, and among those being significant the parameter estimates are generally higher than when doing OLS-regressions.

The conclusion, therefore is, that OLS-estimations as wells as fixed-effect-estimations have their drawbacks, but if one wish to get rid of some unobserved characteristics affecting the transitions between different life-stages fixed effects estimations is the most appropriate estimation method to be used.